TREE FAILURE AND OTHER ADVENT POEMS:

A CONVERSATIONAL LAMENT

KARA DILLOW
SUSAN WIGGIN

PUBLISHED BY:
THE BEACON HILL PROJECT
2025

Published by The Beacon Hill Project
P.O. Box 9001
Asheville, North Carolina 28815
www.thebeaconhillproject.com
Instagram: @thebeaconhillproject2025
Substack: thebeaconhillproject2025

ISBN 979-8-9935531-0-8
Subject: Poetry; Asheville, NC; Hurricane Helene
Authors: Dillow, Kara; Wiggin, Susan

Design by Robert Bradley
Cover tree illustration: Susan Ruth Wiggin Mueller

Printed in the United States of America

First Edition December 2025

A percentage of the proceeds of
Tree Failure and Other Poems: A Conversational Lament
to benefit The Arbor Day Foundation at www.arborday.org.

"If You Are a Poet," translated by Diana Der Hovanessian, is copyright © *Poetry East*
#110, Fall 2024, edited by Richard Jones. Reprinted by permission of *Poetry East*.

*Dedicated to the kind and steadfast people of Buncombe County
in the Blue Ridge Mountains of Western North Carolina,
who endured, who endure, who will endure.*

If You Are a Poet

Gevorg Emin

Don't blink.
The people's eyes stare
out of your eyes.

Don't be silent.
You are the word upon
your country's lips.

Don't turn your head.
You may miss
history's secret voice.

If you are not time's sacrifice
how can you witness the miracle
of resurrection?

You do not own the right
to bow your head.
You have to see
what is coming.

The true poet, are you?
Then carry your century's burden
even if the weight kills you.

"If You Are a Poet," translated by Diana Der Hovanessian, is
copyright © *Poetry East* #110, Fall 2024, edited by Richard Jones.
Reprinted by permission of *Poetry East*.

CONTENTS

Introduction | 3

Conversational Prompt	*Kara Dillow*	*Susan Wiggin*
External		
Winter	12	First Frost	Advent
Bare Winter Trees	16	Christmas Trees	Splinter
Fire + Darkness	22	Hearth	Stoke
Snow	26	Glitter: A Haiku	Flurries
Red Berries	28	Hope Waiting	Red Berries
Debris	30	Debris	Tree Failure
Play	34	Childishness	Touché
Salvage	38	The Dump	The Remnant
Curate	44	Thank you, Andrew	These Days
Internal		
Gesture	50	Hurt	Wait For It
Rest	52	Baby Bear	Hibernation
Vibration	54	After	Kindred Roots
Breath	58	On Edge	Still
Tradition	62	Relevant	Because
Relations	66	Empathy	Generations
Stay	68	Learning	Ode To The Trees
Annoyance	70	Too Much	Fleeced
Eternal		
Content	74	Letting Go	The Christmas Gift
Transience	78	Wait	Journey
Fertile	82	Bittersweet	Expectant
Ponder	86	Hole	Frank
Hope	88	The Cardinal	Carol
Receive	92	Natural Math	The Giver
Rebirth	96	Overdue	Rural Renewal
Courage	98	Super Heroes	Fear Not

TREE FAILURE AND OTHER ADVENT POEMS:

A CONVERSATIONAL LAMENT

I do not remember when it started raining, maybe the rain began Wednesday or Thursday as Hurricane Helene approached. It was late September of 2024, and I drove down to the Swannanoa River one night, about a mile from our house, tucked up and away in a small neighborhood called Grovemont, to take a picture so that in the morning we could tell how much the river had risen with all the rain before and during Hurricane Helene. Watching her rise to the lip of her banks year after year and storm after storm, was a reminder of the power of nature. No one expected what would happen in the next 24 hours in Western North Carolina, in the mountains surrounding the highly visited tourist destination of Asheville and its small surrounding towns.

On Friday September 27th, it was still raining, and it was windy. Hurricane Helene was upon us.

In Swannanoa, we have had "hurricane" wind and rain before, but it was never more than a mildly heightened storm. We are 6 hours from the coast, and most often, hurricanes blow through fairly unremembered. My family, my husband and my two pre-teen sons, our dog and cat, and I all stayed home that day. Our whole area had lost power, and no one went to work. Our small backyard had over six inches of water and more that poured in, like a waterfall, from the mountainous neighborhood behind us. Our driveway became its own river. When it rains in the mountains, it's like being at a water park. All the water flows and funnels downhill and gathers and gathers until it hits a river, reservoir, or lake. We heard the roads were too dangerous, but the news had not even begun to trickle in to tell us of what was truly transpiring, nor did we have the power or service to hear much of anything anyways. We had all made it through a couple days with no power from wind or ice before. You get out all the board games and a good book you've been meaning to read along with the old candles for the evening, and like camping, you go to bed not long after sunset. Everything slows down and is much quieter. Still, I remember flushing the toilet for the final time when the water didn't come back. We had never lost water like this before. The water would not return for several weeks. We would be two months without potable water of our own!

Friday, late morning, my younger son was anxious. He is a Covid kid, which means he spent two years mostly at home, away from school and friends, being just old enough to know what was happening out in the world but not quite able to understand it. He no longer liked to be trapped at home. The rain was letting up, so I told him we should go for a walk. "Let's go see what trees fell and how much the river rose."

These are the moments when time stands still, and what you see is seared into your brain forever. We have three exit points from Grovemont, all of which are along old US 70 which runs right along the Swannanoa River. My son and I walked to each of these points and saw that all three were flooded with the raging Swannanoa River or a tributary. Houses were consumed, and some of them had people in them. A little girl waved at me from her bedroom window while water consumed her house on all sides. People stranded on rooftops screamed for help. Everyone who could was out walking, back and forth, trying to make sense of what we all saw. Shock and disbelief were evident on everyone's face. We all knew this was bad, really bad. My son and I walked eight miles that day in a daze. The only other way out would be on foot over the mountains to the north of us, but that was mostly wilderness and would not be an option.

Flood water is scary. It moves very quickly. It is cutting new paths all the time as the water finds its way of least resistance. You can't quite tell how deep it is, except for using reference points, like homes and businesses that it has engulfed. The more dangerous part is what the water carries from upriver: swaths of industrial plastic, sharp pieces of metal ripped from structures, broken and splintered trees, oil tanks, storage containers from semi-trucks, debris from roads and homes, and whole houses. Many people were swept away in those couple of days and lost forever. Many of the carried objects remained in the landscape hauntingly when the waters receded.

All I could think at this juncture, as we realized we were locked in, was how we had not saved enough drinking water, not even for a couple days. How would we get water? We have a creek up the road from our house. We have camping gear. We would get to work and prepare potable water. This would be our main focus for the next 8 weeks. We, as civilized humans, take potable water, power, and fresh perishable food for granted. I never realized how access to healthy water is central to our entire existence: drinking, cooking food, washing hands, showering. Our grocery stores were shut down. Our gas stations were closed. We were isolated, desolate, and scared. Finding water would become our full- time job.

After drinking water and food, the next responsibility was extended family. We heard that my husband's parents were safe closer to Asheville in an area called Haw Creek. We rode our bikes 2.5 miles to my parents' house on the other side of the ridge. They had no water and no power either. Their refrigerated food was rotting. The sedentary water in the toilets was becoming ripe. All of their roads were covered in downed trees and powerlines, and there was no way out by car. Neighbors began to chainsaw small pathways and arches through the trees just to check on one another and see what conditions lay on the other side. Those with ATV's and power equipment did what they could. Other main roads were washed away, giant chunks of pavement simply picked up and displaced, or covered in mud too deep and soggy to pass a car. The powerlines draped back and forth across these roads like Christmas garlands. My father, in his late 70's, could not walk a mile off the mountain let alone the tenth of a mile down his very steep driveway. My husband and son carried him down, and we eventually evacuated him and my mother by car when we were able and drove them safely down to Durham, NC once we had syphoned enough gas from my husband's truck to my Honda Pilot. We began to hear of people desperately needing gas for life support equipment. What was happening?

Once my parents were safe, we were able to regroup, and my family returned to Swannanoa to help our community recover. We would be without power. We would be unable to take showers. We knew we could figure this out, but we needed to be home. We needed to be part of whatever was coming next.

This collection was inspired by the experiences of one small group of people during the immediate aftermath of Hurricane Helene. There are many many more experiences from many more people, and all are needing to be heard or expressed in one form or another. My story was shared with a creative friend, and as we each questioned how to process the trauma, fear, guilt, and hope of living through a natural disaster, as well as watching so many others suffer through loss and recovery, we proposed that writing would help us find our way. We used the time of advent, and for 25 days, we wrote. We offered one another prompts to stir memory and emotion and to invite healing. This collection is an expression of how two humans supported and met one another through grief, awe, and hope, to arrive on the other side of the darkest days of the year with the wish to move forward.

Kara Dillow
Swannanoa, NC

On September 27, 2024, we woke to find that the storm that was supposed to have turned toward Atlanta before hitting Western North Carolina — because "we never get hurricanes" — didn't. My husband and I had gone to bed aware that the ground was already saturated by days of heavy rain, but secure in both our elevation and the history of storms glancing off the Blue Ridge region that we call home. I had slept lightly, waking with every weather app notification to pray and check the radar image on my phone; a huge red swirl of water-laden clouds barreling straight up through South Carolina before camping out on top of us, bringing too much wind and too much rain. Like a bowling ball in suspended strike, I thought at the time. But they said it would turn....

We threw open the deck doors and rejoiced the morning after — my husband playing the old hymn *Great is Thy Faithfulness* on the piano to the God of our personal pass-over — and set about taking inventory of damage and emergency supplies: water, candles, matches, dog food, protein bars, flashlight, backup batteries, analogue clock, vintage 9v AM transistor radio... check, check, check. (I was a good Campfire Girl back in the day.) We assumed the power would come back on before the plenty of food in the fridge went bad, and if not that the half tank of gas in the car would easily get us to the store and back for provisions if it took a few days to get the grid back up. But that afternoon, while neighbors checked on neighbors, news of just how bad it was down the hill trickled in as folk tried to venture down our cove's single access road only to be turned back by tree-blocked roads and washed-out bridges.

Oh. *That* bad.

We "glamped" in our own home for weeks, eyeing rotting food and dwindling supplies, with no electricity. No running water. No internet or cable and no end in sight. Really? In 2024? In America?

Some days later, once donated *Starlink* hotspots provided our neighborhood with communications hubs at 5pm daily, we tried to explain to those outside the region, that we were recovering from an *actual* disaster because of our unique topography and demographics, and not just weathering another storm. But there is no way to know what its like to see people's inside things outside until you have lived it; not as a newsreel scene of some distant stranger whose losses seemed remote and unimaginable, until now. Tankers aren't supposed to hang in trees, nor are the shattered, twisted, remnants of the every day supposed to be deposited in impossible places by 26' floodwaters, 2000 landslides, tornadic wind sheers that tore and flattened 822,000 acres of tall trees. Not here. Not normally.

What I recall most from those first weeks, outside of the thrumming of a neighbor's generator and rescue helicopters overhead set against the otherwise silent and dark, was the spinning disorientation of constant recalibration as my mind fought to sort and refile the disorder. That and how, in a single day, the most contentious presidential election in memory fell off our collective radar, although just weeks away, while the rest of the country was being whipped toward the polls in a frenzy. We here, rather, sought solid, common ground despite differences and found our footing in relationship and the disturbing reality of human frailty. We were disaster survivors now, banded together against a common existential fear. The cold of winter would soon be upon us and there were thousands suffering in our community; too many still lost, stranded up mountain roads or across bridges that had washed away, or without basic necessities, intact homes and warm beds. As help began to pour in from caring people around the country, strategic political rhetoric sounded tone deaf and irrelevant when it wasn't clear whether or not we'd have polling places or, for some, the means to reach them. No one was asked for proof of political party when they arrived with a generator, or when someone was served fresh water and hot food, or helped to shovel real mud, slung high and wide. We were talking across mended fences again in ways that we hadn't since the pandemic response of 2020 divided relationships and damaged economies. Helene was no friend to southern Appalachia, but she brought us back together again, fiercely, and we remembered why it was good to be kind. We pressed into love-thy-neighbor as neither political divisiveness nor the natural world's unpredictability could top our common need to see and to speak hope.

The news trickling in daily was ugly; loss piled upon loss of property, association, routine, and beautiful, historic terrain eclipsed only by the loss of life to flood and landslide. And then there were the very real economic ripples affecting the lives and livelihoods that make up our largely hospitality-based economy. It was shocking, really. And that we were; in shock, as we mucked out the aftermath — physically, mentally, emotionally — blinking against the stunning realization of how tenuous are our lives, and how fragile the illusion that we could hold at bay the natural order and chaos of creation. We found ourselves collectively disordered, and more than usually aware of the deeper blow to those among us who, on a good day, walk a thin line along the edges of productive citizenship. It was up to those who could to hold the hope for those who were struggling to keep, or pull it, together, or who simply had to move on to find work while the region navigated a recovery that would take years.

But after shock comes acceptance, resolve and, in these parts, grit. Mountain folk do more than survive the creek rising and the mud and the mud and the mud, they dig in and out and do what needs doing. Together. In the stripping away of our riparian banks and surrounding topsoil, the flood had revealed deep, abiding roots from which the region began to reweave its fabric. All around us, as in generations past, eyes lifted up off of the wreckage to the mountains that we call home and beyond to find hope in the God who made them. True to its live-and-let-live social contract, the Asheville region, surrounding watershed and forested lands, pulled together at the oars of rescue, recovery and the re-establishment of home.

As the leaves fell and Thanksgiving approached, I considered the deep wounds revealed and darkening days and wondered how will this community manage a winter season normally brightened by holiday observances and family traditions? Could we muster the same gratitude, cheer, comfort and joy going on around the world when the new year held for us more difficult recovery and layers of loss we'd just begun to realize? When Kara was able to reopen her Pilates studio in early December, we regulars were grateful for a return to some routine and self-care. We stumbled into winter by this meager light of hope, the warmth of belonging stirring in us an inner thaw in defiance of the growing cold outside. And as our region rallied, a broader, uniquely Ashevillian conversation also emerged through varied worldviews and perspectives. Expressive voices became the vibrant colors of weft woven across the stationary, vertical warp of history, traditions, geography and creation's seasonal rhythms.

It was in this spirit of compassionate collaboration — each viewing the same event through a different lens — that Kara, a lover of the natural world raised in Swannanoa, and I, a Boston-born follower of Jesus Christ, would exchange poetic responses to the tragedy of Hurricane Helene; sharing our common love for creation, grieving together over the violent damage that nature had both wrought and sustained, and gathering hope as it — as we — began to heal. Living east of Asheville, my home close to the massive tree loss in Pisgah Forest and Kara's in the path of deadly mudslides and the turned out Northfork Reservoir, we initially had no words to describe what we were witnessing. Both writers, we agreed that if we were struggling to process and voice our traumatic experience, what of those who were not people of words? What creative responsibility did the expressive artists, writers and musicians who call these Mountains home bear to mark the meaning of this life-altering event for each other, our neighbors, for the region and the historical record? We couldn't just move on. The trees needed mourning. The uncounted lives lost needed marking. Things needed saying.

And so this poetry project grew out of conversations between friends seeking light at a dark moment in time, seeing the same hard thing from different perspectives and processing in respectful, creative dialogue. We chose the annual season of Advent, December 1st-25th, to consider both *creation* and *Creator*: Kara sharing observances of the annual winter Solstice as the seasonal return of the sun to warm the earth and bring anew the perpetual cycle of fruit and harvest; and myself anticipating the coming Christ, God in flesh, who made both sun and fruit and breaks the power of darkness in human hearts. By Christmas, we had 50 poems; a time capsule of storm recovery, of neighbor helping neighbor and strangers pressing in, of life going on, and kindness flowing like tankers full of free, fresh water. The prompts and poems took us deep into the dark and hard, then wheeling back out to the light of solace and peace. Words became for us the restoration of order within and around us, as we teased out memories and shaped meaning, splattered with mud and tears and, gratefully, laughter. We found that true restoration is in what holds mankind together; far more life-giving than the allegiances and differences that threaten to tear us apart.

It slowly became safe to relax again, to breathe easy, and at last to mourn. I wrote in lament, as Autumn's camouflage fell away and our forest's bruised and broken bones lay ravaged in the gray. And as I lifted my heart to the One who made it to mend and to fill, it was with a clear sense of purpose to then, in turn, fill and mend from His eternal bounty.

As I write this, at the first anniversary of the storm and flood response, we are just now beginning to see the fruit of restorative expression that will unfurl for years to come as we are, after all, created creative in the image of the Creator. Kara and I join an armada of creative community response that began at dawn on September 27, 2024, knowing at the start it would rise and carry through our recovery because how could it not? Our small contribution to this regional project begins with this collection of poetic laments, now entered into what is becoming an artistic historical record as rich and fertile as the topsoil Helene washed away. May these conversations help to restore and seed the new common ground on which we find ourselves; establish strong roots of understanding and dialogue; bridge the divide of difference with humility, compassion and true justice; celebrate diversity of thought and expression by which we recognize our unique humanity and interconnectedness; and steward well the land we only imagine we can own or control as part of a robust and diverse ecosystem designed for such a time as this by the loving hand of the Creator who is not surprised by any of it.

This collection of poems is an unlikely skiff, but I have been buoyed by it. My hope is that it might serve others where they are — adrift, becalmed, lost in high waters, knee deep in mud — seeking words of life and courage for the journey.

Here are some.

Susan Wiggin
Asheville, NC

External

First Frost

Kara Dillow

It's that time of year again,
the first frost.
The leaves have fallen
from our massively old oaks trees
that loom over our very average house,
and they have filled the driveway
      and frozen to the pavement,
      forming an unbreakable crust.
I half-heartedly attempt to rake into them.
I give up immediately for what seems a futile exercise.
It will take a whole Saturday afternoon
      to rake,
      and scrape,
      and move the mass
      down the hill into the woods.
I see the dahlias in the garden have frozen,
and their beautiful color-filled heavy heads
are drooping like ragdolls
on slimly sewn bodies,
and as they begin to thaw into pulp in the mid-morning sun,
I decide that it's time
to cut them back,
      dig up their tubers,
      and store them in the garage,
until summer comes
and sunflowers bloom high,
and bees float from disc to disc.
Soon, it will be time to cut winter greens
and time to make wreaths,
and give gifts,
forage for red berries
      and pinecones,
      and new evergreens,
and colorful things.

The world will come alive again,
a winter garden.
It's this time of year
when the woods speak
in a new way,
as a pond freezes,
as the sap descends,
not so unlike a cat stretching from a nap
on a sunny pillow.
The squirrels play and hunt, chittering and
carrying nuts to secret holes all their own,
planning for the shorter colder days,
and in the grass, the birds enjoy a rarer
morning sunbath,
such a sweet gift from the sky,
occasionally, on these colder days.

Advent

Susan Wiggin

Thin, crisp sunlight barely reaches the frozen ground.
Barely warms the skin. Barely stirs the heart.
The time has come to slow down. Tuck in. Take stock.
To measure the impact of our effort and
Pause —
Pondering loose ends. Loss. Death, searching shadows
For new life to follow, surely, by design.

We draw inside, weaving cocoons of comfort against cold,
Hard edges,
And pull close our plans. Our people. Our ideas and dreams.
We quiet our thoughts
And make soup.
Banked against the chill,
We exhale and begin the wait.

We wait for hope;
    not dry, but thirsting still in this mean time.

We wait with hope;
    stoking one another's anticipation.

We wait by hope;
    provisioned, we've got this. We do.

We wait in hope;
    because roots gather strength in rest.

The fall reveals our loss and the dark road ahead.
Yet we hope,
The remnant,
For return. For Light.

Christmas Trees
Kara Dillow

Part 1

It is only the first week of December,
and we have set up the Christmas tree.
We buy a big expensive one now,
and we enjoy it as long as possible
(just after Thanksgiving).
The tree fills up the front window
of the living room,
and we considered how it looks
from the outside,
like some Christmas post card.
Still,
this feels like being a kid again,
as we
head to the tree market excitedly and,
as a family,
walk down rows of cut trees:
spruce, fur, pine.
And, oh, the smell of cut trees is deep,
brought down from Watauga county.
Our banter begins.
This one is the tallest,
widest,
fullest,
sturdiest…
Magically, everyone agrees on the final one to come home.

We unwrap our tree in the house,
put it in its dirty sap-stained tree stand,
adjusting by degrees to looks straight enough,
drag out the decorations from the attic
and spend one lovely evening
drinking watered down hot chocolate
together as a family,

listening to the same Christmas songs
we will hear a thousand times
over the season,
and pulling out 20 years' worth of memories
in ornaments
before children and after children and so on.
First Christmas's and first homemade decorations.
Then, even better, the next morning,
it's cold outside, very cold,
And there is snow on the ground,
like an electric fence that says,
"Stay, go no farther,
go sit on the couch."
School is cancelled!
I stay in my pajamas and slippers
for one more hour.

Part 2

On this cold snow-covered December morning,
instead of running out the door racing
kids to school,
speeding mindlessly off to work
on the winding back roads, I could now drive in my sleep,
I make a fresh hot cup of Irish breakfast tea.
I find a cozy corner on the loveseat.
I begin to write,
needing to remember this feeling,
and I admire our sweet tree,
the one that the whole family agreed upon,
shrouded in bright LED lights,
dressed in our years of memories and milestones.
I flip the switch to the
fake gas fireplace
to add a layer of ambience and nostalgia,
and I sit and look,
longer than I normally give myself permission
to be still.

Our tree looks entirely loved,
Wrapped in our life stories.

Yet, the bare winter trees outside
creep in with a whisper,
And my attention shifts
out the living room windows,
past our shrouded tree.

Part 3

Western North Carolina,
and we are two months out from the storm and the floods from Helene.
Time doesn't move forward the same in a place like this now.
Our trees were ripped up and torn away,
and so many lives stopped.

The Swannanoa River is close,
and I can see down through the valley
where I couldn't used to be able to see
because there used to be woods,
bare winter trees in the cold morning sunrise,
some still standing,
tall and straight in
the soft silver pink of the waking horizon,
naked and shifting under the bite of the winter breeze,
out there,
as the day just begins
to open its eyelids.

I think of the folks
living in tents on the river now,
neighbors who lost everything
but who will stay on their land,
who will rebuild their lives slowly.

They will be up and about this morning,
in hats and gloves,

making hot breakfasts on camp stoves.
They will mill about their river encampments
as the sun finishes its morning climb,
where they hold their ground.
I wonder if they too are getting ready for work.

My tree, decked in LED lights,
fades into the pale-yellow morning beam of the windows.
It is one of the coldest mornings we have had yet,
and after a time
the window is too bright,
and I am blinded.
I can hardly see the room or
my Christmas tree.

Splinter

Susan Wiggin

You almost have to look away.
Almost.
Exposed, they appear; naked in the early snow.
Broken. Suspended. In a dance of impossible angles.
That's not right, you whisper. And yet it is.
You drive by.
The violence of it frozen in time, too much to absorb.

And you drive by.
And you drive by.
And they stand. And bend. And twist and
reach. Shattered, yet they stand. For now.
Defying gravity as if in flight.
Rooted. Still and strong. You hope.
Like me, in this after. You pray.

And you drive by.
And there's something obscene
about their brokenness.
As if held in the spotlight.
Caught in the act.
Moaning, "nothing to see here." "Move on."
And we will.

Some day, when they are gone
or we stop looking for splinters,
we will also remember the day
before, when they stood
tall and proud,
wind in their branches, reaching
for stars.

Hearth

Kara Dillow

I am wondering about the first peoples,
as I snuggle by my nighttime lamp,
under my big comforter,
in this winter season when the nights are long
and
when the nights are very cold.

What stood between *them*
and the slow, deathly sleep
of freeze?
A small fire, mere coals,
maybe an animal skin cover,
and a small wet cave or meagre mud encrusted hut?
How the wind must have howled?
It aches in my bones.

How far we have come.
How far have we come?

Even not so long ago,
before electric heat and indoor plumbing
and buying cold homogenized pasteurized
skim milk at the grocery store,
recent peoples had no lights to illuminate
after sun set,
and the true northern folks
had only night for half the year.
Cold and dark were normal,
as normal as the sun and heat of day
for people on the equator.
How that must have shaped their very
existence.

I wonder if there such a thing as
Seasonal Affective Disorder?

It could be the compulsion toward winter hibernation
or first world malaise,
existential angst.
Being cold is unpleasant.
It hurts. It's exhausting.
The fireplace,
for first peoples
must have been close to sacred.

How rarely do we appreciate
the flick of a light switch or thermostat,
the rush of fresh running water from our tap.
The flood recently taught us this.

The hearth was the heart of human cultures,
every people,
every village,
throughout time,
from moonrise to moonset,
where people gathered,
        sang,
        cooked,
        slept,
        where people sacrificed in hope that there could be
less pain and suffering,
more ease in their day,
more comfort for their children.
How far we have come.
How far have we come?

Stoke

Susan Wiggin

as the days descend into darkness,
the chill of winter seeps to bone. goosebumps
defy layers of natural fiber and fleece.
it's official: winter.

we withdraw.
pull in. shrink back
from icy hands, no matter
their intention, and slow to a stop.
freeze frame. and... scene.

but (and I say this with great relief) just
when the flesh begins to forget its flush, someone,
kindly, strikes a match, kindles a flame and stokes
the glow of a warming fire just enough
to awaken a dream of sunflowers.

Glitter: A Haiku

Kara Dillow

Snow cuts the sun's light.
Snowflakes, like glitter bombs or
Ninja throwing stars.

Flurries

Susan Wiggin

It snowed, he said. And I roll over.
Not thinking it "real" snow;
Real stick-on-the-ground, better-stay-home,
Make-milky-cocoa kind of snow.
Feathery flakes of angel lint kind of snow
As if heaven is fluffing comforters,
Clothing all the world in white.
Or at least outside my window. In my world.

And for too brief a time,
Here in these scarred and tattered
True blue mountains, beauty flutters
Down like Peace;
Soothing hearts, settling bones,
Slowing pulse and pace
Just enough to toss a blanket
Over all that wood.

Hope Waiting
Kara Dillow

Rose hips,
Holly berries,
and Bittersweet.

Amongst the brown, dull gray,
and barrenness of winter,
the earth gives us this,
in bright red fruit and berries.
like the glimpse of the
crimson cardinal.
There is still hope.
There is still beauty,
and there is still life
deep within, waiting to renew
after a time...

after a time.

Red Berries

Susan Mueller

there! on the snow bank!
impossibly red berries.
the junco will come.

Debris

Kara Dillow

Flood

We build with neat blocks.
Nature has little mercy.
She shreds and splinters.

Piles

Piles of debris,
the edges of all roads home,
mud and stuff, like cookie dough.

Hope

Some days feel despair.
How can people move forward?
Volunteers and love.

Tree Failure

Susan Wiggin

Driving through
remnants of storm, again
I ponder the words of natural disaster.
Compound words, like
TORNADIC SHEERS
FLOOD PLANE
DEBRIS FIELD.
Words that speak of
loss. So much loss.
Such words, drawn from the
special use vocabulary file,
get bandied about
— underlined, italicized, bold —
when one, simple word
can't express the disordered
magnitude of the thing.
Evocative word combinations, like
SHELL SHOCKED
TRAUMA RESPONSE
TREE FAILURE
that, paired, punch high
— in the heart — in the gut —
UTTER CATASTROPHE
WAR ZONE
TOTAL DEVASTATION
and reference a breach, not easily repaired
without something to hold it together.
Hold it together.

Rerouted, I weave around mounds
and imagine we'll soon stop seeing the
wreckage. Stop hearing the wind
when it howls, and the rain
when it pelts the windows.

We'll stop noticing the water
rise silty, insistent, streaming
across the road. So much water...

Perhaps we'll stop seeing, hearing,
feeling the tragic too much of it
once the debris is hauled
off to elsewhere, and nature restores
itself, as it will do, reclaiming its mighty
fallen back to landscape; once we lift
our eyes from mud to mountain
we'll remember
that words also heal, like
SURVIVAL INSTINCT
PULLING THROUGH
COME BACK
and that the greatest healing of all
rests still in the hand of the
One who conceived of seed.

Childishness

Kara Dillow

We humans take ourselves
too seriously.
Where was the email
from above
that life has to get harder
as we get older.
We only have value if
we are agitated?
Be productive
and squeeze every last
second out of every single day,
until there is no fun left,
and fill every moment with
work and chores.
My adult years
will be spent,
until they are all gone.

Why can't we just
play?
I want to climb trees then see
if I can balance on my hands,
and then do cartwheels in the grass.
Can I get lost
in the woods and see
if I can find my way home?
I want to binge on wild
raspberries
then lay all afternoon
in the shade of a beautiful tree
and watch the clouds turn
from turtles to
dogs to nonsense and
nothing.
Silly, maybe, and

even I know that,
but I want to keep a tender
hopeful heart
that life can still be
whatever I want it to be.

I want to feel
that each day still
has unknown potential
because the world is a good place,
and people are nice.
Most of the big dreams and
exciting plans are still
awaiting me,
and it's OK because
I am still deciding who I want
to be when I grow up.

Touché

Susan Wiggin

Once freed from jobs and tasks
By machines, precise and efficient,
Will mankind spend surplus time at play?
And will it be just a matter of time, then, before
Machines are developed to play for us as well?
What, then, shall we do but long for work?

The Dump
Kara Dillow

My mother raised 5 children
In the 1980's
In rural New England,
Two girls and three boys.
She had one grocery store
30 min away.
We had one TV,
With three television stations,
ABC, PBS, and...
Well maybe just two.
Sesame Street was all
I remember watching then
And playing with Barbies.
We had one telephone
(With a cord).
Friends had to call
And ask permission to talk to you.
No Target, no Walmart,
No Amazon,
No cell phones,
No devices,
No internet.
We had an Atari,
And you could
play Pac Man
with a joystick.
We had a yard.
We had trees,
Lots of trees,
Limitless woods.
And, well,
We had each other.

My mother was practical,
Minimalist.

She still is.
No makeup,
Tidy.
She believes home is where you rest.
Outdoors is where you live
And work.
She always had us outside.
She was always outside,
Unless she was loading laundry,
And she was often loading laundry
Or cooking dinner.

As we got older,
We were still outside
Always
In the woods,
The children together.
Siblings, cousins, the neighbors up the road.

Yes,
This is intensely nostalgic.
I thought that this is how everyone lives.
"This is forever."
This was reality for us then.
There was nothing else,
And there was no other way.
We were the kings and queens
Of our own imaginations.

My mom always had a yard project.
She was always a slim woman,
But from years of carrying children
And hauling rocks around,
As I now know was just intense
Mental therapy for her,
She always had sculpted biceps.
I laugh because
She was embarrassed by them.

Muscles like that weren't attractive!

We got presents on our
Birthdays and Christmas.
Christmas was magical, truly.
The lights, opening one or two presents.
The smells, the music, and the snow,
Real build-a-snowman-kind-of-snow,
Getting to see all the aunts and uncles
And cousins who lived around us
But not near us.
Magic.

We were not spoiled but
Would get a new outfit
For school.
I remember that dress with the pink ribbon
When I started third grade.
We got a pencil at the dentist
With our name carved into it
With the dentist drill, twice per year.
We got a McDonald's hot fudge Sundae
Once a summer.

When I was 6 or 7
Years old
My dad got us a VCR
And there was one VHS
Rental place a couple towns over,
So once a week
We started to
load up in the station wagon
and rent a video.
My mom locked her keys
In the car once there.
Mom called dad from the video store,
And we had to wait for him
To unlock the car.

He was not happy.
He was never happy.
That's another story.
"She always did this,"
He'd say.
She put up with a lot from him.
Too much in my opinion.

Her job was raising children,
And it was 24/7.
She never took a long hot bath,
Had a girls' night out,
Called a sitter,
Or dropped us at
Grandma and grandpa's house,
Who lived a mile away.
She did everything with us
And for us
And thought sitting down
To read a book
Was a luxury.
Again,
That's another story.

We swam in the local lake,
Even when it rained.
We picked wild blueberries
Off the side of the road.
We had picnics.
Climbed apple trees in October.
We took long walks in the woods.
We took longer drives
On winding country roads.
"It's an adventure,"
She would always say.
As a mother,
I know now,
"It's entertaining you,

Isn't it?"
Is what she really meant.

Our town had a local dump
Where everyone took their trash.
I remember piles of junk.
We'd drive over there once per week,
Once per month.
What was time
Back then?
I didn't know that we went there to
Drop trash off.
Sometimes mom was just looking.
She liked to see what people left
To see if she could salvage it.
Clean it up,
Refinish it…
Furniture, toys especially.
One New Englander's junk
Was my mom's new project.
She was good at
Seeing the potential
In what others discarded,
Believed that if something worked
Or functioned good enough
You kept using it,
Even if it was hard.
She was good
at making due with what she had,
Even if it was hard,
Filling up our days with new experiences
And unplanned challenges.
She still is.

The Remnant

Susan Wiggin

Out of what's left,
we find our way.
From the mud and
Ash arises what will be.
What was is not.
What is will become
What it was always
Meant to be.
Even this.

On shadows and
Dreams, we stand,
Knee deep, reaching
For hope and finding
Hands reaching
For hope. Out of
What's left, we
Find one another.
And this is enough.

Thank You, Andrew

Kara Dillow

He
Is deeply intent on doing good.
He
Works to undo the selfish and ignorant things
That other people do,
And he does it because
It is what needs to be done.
He participates in
Community events that
Make the world a better place.

There is no glory for him,
No expectation of gratitude,
Maybe just a look
And a nod of understanding
That this is
All
Our work to do,
Together,
To make this place better than
When we found it
And to leave it the best it can be
For those that follow.
Don't take,
Give.

And in these dark days,
And in this season of slumber,
He had a tree lit in the center
Of all the mud and all the disaster.
One you can see from all the corners of wreckage
And through all the debris-filled trees
And demolished businesses.
He
Pulled the pieces together

And found the people and the parts
That could do the thing.
Like a museum director curating
A seasonal gallery,
He gave us
A picture of hope
Because it is what needed to be done.

These Days

Susan Mueller

And so it comes.
The air turns brisk and dry, the leaves dry and fall and
Fall, begun in joy and lush chroma, crumbles at our feet.
But we do not mourn, much. For without such
passings, there would be no beginnings;
no sweet Spring to advance beyond itself to Summer
splendor, and no ripening toward the reaping of harvest.

Such is the certain work of the hours; passing,
predictably, longest to shortest to longest, with
variation in experience alone. We would curate
nature's march of days, but the gallery of time —
each moment, mounted or framed — is a gift
for those who set their life by its rhythmic
patterns and seek cosmic order over chaos.

Fertile fields recede to fallow. The season
of reclamation and rest settles to sweet wintertide
— all tucked in and turned down — while
every passing hour, as sure as the sun, anticipates
restoration. Resurrection's sure rise.
Once and again.

"Let there be light."
And there was... is... will be.
And so it goes.

Internal

Hurt

Kara Dillow

A gesture is worth a thousand words.
When you turn away from me,
glance away, for
an imperceptible split second,
shoulders slightly tensed,
as I sum up my day to you
and work for an intimate moment,
but you display a lack of interest
or concern
briefly
you convey a lack of desire
for me.

You didn't even notice.

I did.

Wait For It

Susan Wiggin

I await a whisper. Perhaps
an eyebrow, barely lifted. A nod of ascent.
The upturned corner of a well-lined lip.

I sit stock still for hours, I'm sure, looking for a sign.
A gesture. Anything to indicate that
the time has come. *My* time. At last.

Inquiry hangs suspended like
Mistletoe; pregnant with anticipation
And something else. Dread? Can one die of dread?

I press my tongue against my teeth and exhale.
Had I ever exhaled before? And what is a "hale" anyway?
How long without oxygen before braincells die?

Do zombies eat brains if they're dead? I wonder
Would they would use a spoon or a straw?
Probably plastic, either way.

And then — sharp intake of breath — she looks
Up and over her horn-rimmed glasses.
Right. At. Me.

There it is, at last. The Sign. I lurch
Up and over to the cold marble counter,
Averting eye contact with anyone resembling a zombie,

Plant my feet, peel apart cracked lips, and
Croak from parched throat,
"License renewal."

Baby Bear

Kara Dillow

Neighborhood bears,
in these mountains,
are part of the territory.

There's a baby black bear
we see among the trees
when we walk our hound dog
along our backroads.
He's roaming around alone,
too young to be by himself.
He lost his mother in the storm,
we think.
How sad.
We noticed him in October and
were glad for days a bit too
warm and dry for this time of year,
hoping he'd get a little more time,
a little more food,
grow a little older
a little fatter,
before the cold long nights
of December and January.
I've been making sure my compost pile
is full without regret.

We hope he has found a place
to tuck himself in when he needs
to stay warm,
inside a great pile of leaves and debris.
Poor guy.

We hope he makes it through the winter
and we see him in the spring,
eating bear corn and grubs
and tearing up our neighbors' trash.

Hibernation

Susan Wiggin

Weary to the bone.
This pillow. It's so fluffy.
Just close my eyes for

After

Kara Dillow

After an event
a place holds that experience,
like the grand finish of an orchestra.
The room is still full of its vibration.
Maybe that's what spirit is,
the resonance of us
when our physical body is gone.
Each piece of our story left somewhere like a chord.
There is an amount of time after someone leaves
that you can still feel her essence.

I have felt that precious moment before,
when we put our dog down a few years ago.
I felt the moment his life was gone from his body,
untethered,
like a wire disconnected from the battery.
But maybe he was still in the room.
When you drive by a car accident,
you can still feel the moment of their impact, like a struck drum,
even though you didn't witness it
or experience it,
and yet you tense and cringe in contraction.

There was a landslide in our neighborhood,
during the storm,
a big one,
the kind that pulls down three houses
and takes away
everything,
cars, driveways, lives,
and leaves a massive scar.
When you walk by there a few times,
it hurts.
My guts, my bones hurt when I'm there,
in that scar.

I feel their screams,
their panic,
their regret,
the collisions,
their fear,
their moment of realization
and saying good-byes
and frustration that this is how it ends.

The mud and trees
hold their final songs,
like a music box
wound tight and then
to be slowly unwound,
in time,
the tone deepening
and the frequency widening
until it is gone
or simply unrecognized
anymore
by our ears.

Kindred Roots

Susan Wiggin

You could almost hear them;
the mountains, so blue they cried
out to their lost fellows
their vibrational keen echoing
down hollers, rattling the
gaps between what was and
what remains. Strong and stoic
they stood against the clearing
sky, as much of what had
taken generations to be simply was
no more. The mountains had
seen it come and watched it go
again and again.

I *felt* the grief of trees.
A stunned silence that
screamed across
the scarred valley;
something akin to shock,
absorbed and vented,
sending leaves quaking without
a breeze. What remained to
bravely perform the ritual of Fall,
fell; dappled, dancing, but
sad, like tattered tears shed for
one final curtain call.

The trees still aren't talking.
Perhaps they whisper to one another;
intimate, underground
relations, the evidence of which
we can now see scattered across
the landscape — telling tales
of kindred roots wrenched from
the earth and tossed,

indelicately exposed,
still clinging to the soil
that once held them fast
as if to cover the shame of their
muddy tutus,
petticoats it's
impolite to mention.

On Edge

Kara Dillow

At some point
we all learn to hold our breath
to bite our tongue
to not say what we meant to say
because it can't be unsaid.
We unlearn how to ask for
what we need
and we wait for someone to guess,
and we wait for someone to care enough
to tell us to exhale.

Still
Susan Wiggin

Who knew the scent of destruction would be pine?
Or at least it was that morning when I first noticed
its icy clean aroma as the sun returned and we
threw open the doors and sang hymns of gratitude
and hope for the pass over. For the waters' crest.
For another day.

We filled our lungs with herbaceous freshness
mingled with wet earth and something... dank.
And sad. So unlike mountain air in Autumn.
I exhaled. And thought I'd try again
the next day, once the air had cleared,
and everything was back to normal.

Whatever normal is. Or was. Will be.
Best to just breathe without thinking
about what had vaporized and hung
suspended in thin air, in thick mud
where a foulness, like fungus seeps
into lungs and cracked-open hearts, like mine.

But if the mountains breathe so, then, shall I.
They took the brunt of it; eight hundred and
twenty two thousand acres of our trees
lay at the feet of the uneasy rest.
We cling to that remnant and await restoration.
Pray for the cavalry that will not come. But, God....

—

The evening air descends to holler,
drawing up its milky sheets, bedding
down with the damp and the
fumes and the who knows what all else
lingered in that mist.

Lingers, still.

Hardly taking up my space I lay, breath
shallow and sleep
illusive as will-o'-the-wisp,
hoping that the bottom we've hit
will hold. Will cradle weary feet.
To rest. To stand.

We await the dawn, the mountains,
the air and I.
For the sun's sure return will
lift us to the warming
heights, for the breathing of
goodness and the lighting
of dark dreams from which we
once again can see —
as a hawk, circling thermals —
our way clear to the horizon and
the coming day.

Relevant

Kara Dillow

Traditions are thrust upon us by
generations
of grandparents and aunts
who have done things
a certain way,
a very specific way,
year after year,
and their mothers before them
and on and on,
connecting us to elders
and ancestors,
rituals and practices
that can give a sense of
purpose,
a piece of where we have come from
and where we are going.
Yes.

But traditions may
begin to feel like…
a hat
that has grown too small,
a dress that has suddenly become
too tight
and stifling,
out of style,
moth-eaten
and just not relevant
anymore.

Relevance is key.

We are not our parents.
These inherited practices
must change

and evolve
to stay relevant.
Songs should be resung
with new words and verses,
recipes rewritten
and made with,
and played with…
better ingredients
tethering the old to the new and
the past with the future,
respecting wisdom and history,
honoring the elders
yet
appreciating the naïveté and whimsy
of the children.
There is optimism and hope.
There is potential.
Traditions
can be improved
and move us forward.

We have much to learn from one another.

Remember

Susan Wiggin

That's how we do it.
Always has been, and will be.
The Who is the why.

Empathy
Kara Dillow

Empathy is a curse.
We try to teach compassion.
We tell our children to be sympathetic.
Walk one mile in someone else's
sneakers.
But feeling all the feels,
especially everyone else's and
being able to relate to all humans
(and animals)
in every situation and circumstance
is destructive
and debilitating,
like walking along an electric fence
and keeping your finger on the wire.
I will never say,
"I am an empath."
It is not a superpower.
It's called "being sensitive,"
to the point of not knowing
what is yours and
what is theirs.
It's exhausting.
And my great big heart is very tired.

From now on,
I will learn to be
cold and cavalier.
Narcissism sounds so easy.
Self-involvement sounds so relaxing.
Ignorance is Bliss for a reason.

Generations

Susan Wiggin

In consideration of these roots we share
with those on our family tree;
by blood or by choice, we perch on our branches
and wonder, how did we get here.
What began it all? What of its end? And
do we remain here by the power of
deep, mutual connection or trauma bond?

How can relationships — propped and pruned by
holiday, milestone, scandal, celebration, tragedy —
survive the press of time? Or the pull of something more
or less. We are led to shred and shatter mirror images
of one another in this season of deconstruction,
recasting the human drama a farce while the
Author steps out for popcorn.

It will be a miracle, should we survive the
catastrophe/entropy/atrophy of modern
culture and the heavy step of advancing civilization.
For that which is not tightly tied or deeply rooted tends
to run off, be cast aside, or simply drift.
We are lost, again, along our way to reclaim paradise,
holding one another lightly and the world for dear life.

Learning

Kara Dillow

She spent years learning
How to undo her own nature.
As a child,
She was too sensitive and shy
And cried easily when
Her father got angry.
Be more confident.
Be more aggressive.

She was chubby and plain.
She enjoyed daydreaming and music
And taking long walks with her best friend.
Lose weight.
Boys don't like fat girls.

In college, she cared about grades
And wanted to study and travel.
So she did.
Other kids thought she was strange
Or boring
Because she didn't smoke or drink
And stay out late and party,
She tried to exercise and eat right.
She loved to dance, but
She stayed inside alone
Or in the library working on her papers
And taking quick naps.
She learned to write and love poetry.

Later,
Becoming a woman,
She lived a little more,
She wrote more poetry
And listened to her heart.
She moved away from the voices that made her feel unseen
And decided to unlearn her unlearning
And stay as she was.
She loved poetry, and
She began to love herself.

Ode To The Trees

Susan Wiggin

But wait.
I would have them stay.
I would hold on. Hold on.
Hold, please.
Just like that. How it's been.
How it was.
I would keep.
I would linger.
I would steep.
I would tempt with treats.
And try to be worth it.
A hedge against. A stand for.
I'd stop it up. Put a cork in it.
Lock it up
And toss the key.

But, going happens, she said.
Loss is the thing that reveals
The gravity of having had.
Hold lightly, child, to what you
Hold most dear, and trust
That the missing, the fear,
The regret, the lament,
Washes.
Over.
And out.
For now is not forever,
And each now, each
Present, is a gift.
Even this one.
Even this one.

Too Much

Kara Dillow

I have so much to do,
And the dog is whining for a walk.
I have so much to do,
And the alarm is going off to pull the pizzas
Out of the oven for dinner.
I have too much to do, and the cat
Is scratching at the door for his dinner
And
No one has done the dishes
And my oldest needs a form signed for his trip.
My husband needs his button sewn on his dress shirt.
My youngest wants to tell me about his gingerbread house,
And the work emails keep beeping at me.
I left my phone on my desk at work, and
What is my schedule tomorrow?

I didn't eat any fruits or vegetables today.
Did I eat today or drink any water?
Did I go for a walk yet,
Or maybe that was yesterday?
What day is it?

Maybe I'll just have another cup of coffee.
        I have to buy wine for the Christmas party
    And call the veterinarian before the office closes
        And get that follow up at the orthodontist.
Maybe we can avoid braces for another year.
Are those cramps, am I having cramps?
I'll have to run to the store…

Did my sister need me to grab her kids tomorrow?
I'll have to call her before she goes to bed.

I wonder how my mom's skin cancer surgery went…

And the dog is still whining
And the cat is still scratching
And this poem is not going to write itself.

Fleeced

Susan Wiggin

Seriously.
In one day.

One day?
Seriously!?

We send them;
lambs to the slaughter,
to represent the flock.
Full of hope and hubris.
But with plenty of empty yet, to fill
with hooks and sticky wickets;
attach with strings enough to
turn heads and tie hands.

Just how long does it take
wolves to chew up a fresh faced,
idealistic freshman and spit
him out in some back room, littered
with rank compromise and corruption,
avarice and sloth?
How long to choke down
1600 porcine pages, and
digest well enough for a vote?

ONE DAY!?

Spin your partner.
Sidestep. Slippery slope. Promenade.
Rinse, repeat, roll over.

Eternal

Letting Go

Kara Dillow

If you held Contentment up in a mirror,
What would it look like?
What would you see?
If you held it in your hands,
close to your heart,
what would you feel?
Would it have mass or weight?
Would it have edges like a box or
Curves like a sphere,
Or is it more like a place you would go
Or a person or thing you know,
Something you would share with someone,
something you could drape around your neck
without judgment?

Would contentment be a moment,
fleeting at best,
a hot bath and a glass of wine,
a warm cat purring in your lap?
Contentment would not be a *doing*,
I would think.
Maybe it would be the *finishing*,
The good grade at end of a tough semester
Or the medal at the end of a hard race,
when the job is done.

(Pause for thinking)

Maybe contentment is nothing.
It is a state of...

Peace
Zen

No,
It's not nothing.
It's more like
what is in-between everything. Contentment
is the space,

like the notes between the lines,
or more like the pause between the notes,
however imperceptible,
the moment between moments
where time stops
(and you could fall down a rabbit hole here)
where there is just no time at all
and maybe you mildly forget about your existence all together.

It is the seamless transition
from inhale to exhale,
(now we are on a roll)
the place where the body waits to breathe.

No, even that would be something.

Contentment is the lack of awareness
when we just *are*,
Floating in space
Infinitely observing
timelessly existing
no beginning
no ending
just here
just forever and ever, amen.

When we are more space then stuff.

It is the utter acceptance of what is,
And giving in to… whatever.
The triviality of effort.
The universe unfolds as it would,
no matter.
Acceptance of now.

Contentment is connection to the Divine,
whatever you perceive it to be.
It is the perception
of an answer
to *Why*
and yet
letting go
of really needing to know.

The Christmas Gift

Susan Wiggin

Oh my word.
Just look at all that luscious
meaning hung on intentionally
arranged scratches of black on a page,
  or blue or crimson or whatever
  ink the pen might hold.
   And even that — the holding of ink
    — speaks of a reserve ... containment ...
    potential preserved on, with, for purpose.
    All of those bubbling, brewing
     thoughts straining to spill out and say
      something of note, arranged by the
       hand that holds the pen connected to the
        brain that forms the words and crafts the message.
        It blows the mind and, well...
That's a rabbit trail.

Consider, for example, the word <con>tent,
referring to that which is contained,
 and more than relevant during Santa-daze
  when that jolly construct, fed and fattened
   over a few short centuries, whips up the want and the clamor
    and the longing for more and more;
     for the next new thing and the next.
    What to get, what to give to make
     happy, whole, full. (And refill, free!)
      Batteries not included.
       For surely there's a hole in the bucket.
       In this bag. In that box.
        Each package a promise
         and each stocking bulging with stuffers.
          Stuffing. Stuffed with stuff....
What on earth can satisfy and soothe
the ache of the lie of lack?

Consider, now, the word con<tent>
Referring, simply, to a state of being. Just so.
 Is this not the true promise of Christmas?
  Fear not! Comfort! Joy!
   A season for gratitude, and remembering that
    it's not that thing or this which satisfies, but rather
    He who first fills that filling would fulfill.
     Look up, O my soul! From ravenous appetite
      and grasping hands to embrace sufficiency, at last.
      Surrender the striving and claim the promise of
Peace. Illogical peace.

Wait

Kara Dillow

I.
This will pass,
they say,
Don't blink because
you will miss it.

Either way,
time moves on,
and a feeling, a moment that
could seem like a lifetime,
is gone.

You have a choice to suffer
for the moment
and squeeze your fists tight,
stomp your feet in tantrum.

Hold your breath.
It's your choice.

II.
Try to catch leaves in the wind
and you will always be left
running in circles,
chasing your own tail,
like a fool.

III.
See dragons in the clouds
with elation,
with amazement,
then watch is they drift apart
away into unrecognizable pieces,
but something new will take form
if you will keep watching the sky.

Wait.
The passing of time can be unforgiving
or the greatest gift of all.
Whatever the case,

it blurs,
it erases
and subdues
previous
agitation,
good or bad.
It's numb and indifferent,
Thankfully.

Journey

Susan Wiggin

It can take a while
from here to there.
Between this now and then, or when
a lifetime can pass, or a moment
depending on how eagerly anticipated
the departure. Or the arrival. Or how well
occupied the meantime.
Mean time. Can be.
And while a pastime might be pleasant
it isn't yet, not really, so we're
neither here nor there.
At least for now.

Bittersweet

Kara Dillow

I wanted another child.
I wanted a daughter.
And now I have learned that I am beyond those years,
to even try again,
recently informed by my doctor,
and I am young for the average woman.
It was a bit of a shock.
There has been a mourning period
for my fertility years,
a void that I will never bare life again
or carry a child again in my womb.
I will never nurse a child again
to become a fat little toddler.

Most of all, what I lose
is the hope to have a daughter of my own.

I am grateful for my sons
Who are growing healthy,
becoming kind and gentle men,
my soul's heroes!

I think back to the years of getting to know them,
first when they wiggled and kicked my spleen and ribs
inside my body,
to when they were first placed on my skin
wiggling like bags of bones,
Then they were fat little toddlers,
bouncing their foreheads against walls
and their bottoms against stairs.
I caught them in slight delay
as they learned about physics.
Going from being water-born tadpoles
to muscle-bound diaper-wearing
Gravity-testing little humans,

they are almost young men,
(so fast)
Our lives just a video in timelapse.

This time is bittersweet
because my heart is full,
but there's a small quiet,
deep-lying cave
that has a slow trickling stream of longing,
that weeps slightly,
maybe forever or maybe for one more day,
mourning,
or rather wondering who she would have been and how we would have
been together,
taking our long walks when she needed a mother.

I am pensive and yet gratefully screaming
gratitude from the mountaintops,
my heart sings to the stars.

Expectant

Susan Wiggin

Look, I know how these things work.
I'm innocent but not naive.
And no, not perfect. None are.
But here I am. Willing. Trusting.
Anticipating a miracle.
Who am I to carry such a load?
But not alone. Never alone.
Let it be unto me.

Hole

Kara Dillow

Poetry is the rabbit hole
Of pondering
    Wondering about anything and everything
        (well I can't think of anything just now but anyway)
Poetry is the deep well of
Questioning
    The great abyss of curiosity
        The long winding road of
            Exploration
        The wide crevasse of analysis
            The unknown trail of discovery.
            The wide chasm of feeling.
            The infinite beyond...

Like I said,
Poetry
Is
A bottomless
Pit
Of narcissism.

Frank

Susan Wiggin

In his younger days, he'd have said something.
Especially if something really needed saying.
He really wasn't very good at biting his tongue.
Or biding his time. Or waiting at all. For anything.
Some might have called him impulsive. Or impatient.
But I don't know. I just called him frank.

Nowadays, he is more circumspect. More considerate
Of others, not assuming that just because he's had a
Thought, it's worth sharing. Or that anyone would
Care if he did. Some folk are set, and this much he knows:
"You bang your head against the wall until you're done
Banging your head against the wall."

Besides, some thoughts are too odd to share.
Too selfish or paranoid to release into the open,
Unfiltered, where they might be shot down or dismissed.
Or touch a raw nerve. Words have power, he's discovered.
So he learned to ponder. To pray. And sometimes just
Send himself to bed, and expect new mercies tomorrow.

The Cardinal

Kara Dillow

Once when my friend was very sick,
Not physically,
It wasn't cancer or anything,
I didn't know if I was losing him forever.
He was psychotic,
Suicidal,
which can happen to
The brain when its chemistry
Is simply
off.
When someone is in the midst of psychosis,
It's as if they are fragmenting.
It's like watching a mirror shatter.
Their logic splits from their reason.
Their sense of self is split
Into pieces, and they are mastered by
Fear, anxiety, dread,
hopelessness.
I sat with my friend as he seemed to break,
And tried to hold onto one small string
For him,
To hold all the pieces not together
But
At least not fracturing into uncollectable bits
That could no longer be contained
By his façade,
This glass armor he had worn for so long.

I sat with him
And tried to hold him like one of my children
And hoped that love could be his glue
And that all the love he never got,
All the self-loathing he held for himself
All these years,
I could soothe away and hold him together,
Tie his breaking bits back together.

Later, once he was safe
And being cared for
The world felt different.
I had to wonder if this was the end
Of knowing the friend
I'd always known,
Knowing the person who'd always been
There through everything.
It was like a death of something but not someone,
The loss of a very precious item
You always very much took for granted.

I walked often and long in those times.
It was winter and
Often cold
And the bare trees made me feel less lonely,
Like they too understood
Loss.
And once at sunset
In the cold,
Walking,
I saw a single red cardinal on the
Topmost branch of one of these
Bare trees
in the parking lot
Of the hospital,
And he seemed to watch the sunset with me.
He seemed to be feeling the cold night with me.
He wasn't afraid,
And maybe he knew the sun would rise again,
Maybe not,
And the heat would someday return from the sky,
Or maybe not, but
He never moved.
He just perched radiantly,
And I felt that
I should never give up hope.

Carol

Susan Wiggin

Share the reason to hope that
Tomorrow will come. The sun
Will return. The birds will sing
And find seed.

Share the reason to hope that
Wounds heal and the meek overcome.
That darkness will be broken, every time,
By the Light.

Share the reason to hope that
Love came down to find the lost,
To soften hearts, to renew minds,
And to lead the way.

Natural Math
Kara Dillow

Every relationship has one person who gives
And one person who receives.
It is unsaid
And mostly unknown.
It is the Formula of all Relationships
That has always existed,
Forever and ever in all of time.

The giver/the receiver are irrelevant
As they may switch roles at any time.
The giver may lean toward martyr,
And the receiver may be a narcissist.
But the shifting of roles must
Balance out day-to-day,
Eon-by-eon,
A sharing of give and take,
In any relationship
That will live to see another day.
Opposites must attract,
Or things fall apart.

This rings true through and through:
Romantic or platonic,
Domestic pets and their owners,
Farmers and livestock,
gardeners and their plants,
Birds in the trees,
And fish in the sea.
Everything and everyone
Somewhere and somehow
Relates to another,
Needs an other.
We all must orient to something else,
Creating harmony and balance.
Even Narcissus had a pool of water.

Babies cry and mothers give milk,
And the species survives.
Take a dive into the symbiotic
relationships in nature.
Then dive deeper into the parasitic
Relationships, too.
Harmony saves us.
The other is death.

The Giving

Susan Wiggin

Potential builds within like the drawing back of a great wave
Leaving the beach teeming with mysterious glistening
Creatures who'd rather remain unseen.

Like the caught breath, held, before a baby's cry;
The leopard scrunching back, haunches poised to pounce;
The pitcher's wind up, just before letting 'er rip.

There is power in potential, gathered before release.
That exhilarating moment just before the curtain rises, the needle
Drops, or the early edition hits the newsstand and the worm feasts.

In this world of immediate gratification, we've lost the wonder of
A long drawn out wait. The thrill of anticipation has been replaced
By instant disappointment. Alas.

I remember waking early Christmas mornings, straining to hear
The crackling of a Duraflame™ log on the hearth, Bach's cherished
Oratorio on the phonograph, the exotic smell of bacon whetting the appetite.

Lining up by age at the top of the stairs, we siblings waited in hushed obedience
For the unleashing of the thrillingly rare tsunami of festive consumption that
Spun us, raucous and wild, into unrestrained furies.

By mid-afternoon, sticky bits of tape and paper festooning our feety pajamas,
The CRASH of expectations and blood sugar left us bewildered and a bit sad,
Hoping that next year we'd finally learn the secret to comfort and joy.

Overdue

Kara Dillow

Renewing a library book
Feels a little lazy.
Rather than hunkering down
And finishing the story in two weeks,
Just simply ask for two more weeks.
There is no admitting defeat
And declaring a title unfinished.
And now there's an app.
Re-borrow it from the phone,
Or rather just read it from the phone.
Hopefully, there's no waiting list!

Rural Renewal

Susan Wiggin

From mud we were formed.
Dust and spit.
And from this mud we form, again.
Dirt and tears.
One foot, one hand, one story at a time.
Wiser now, one would think, as
History and nature both cycle in chaos.
We have seen what can't be unseen
And remember, that the tending
And manicuring and savoring
Of moments between disasters
Is an intermission.

And so we pull it together.
And soothe senses and souls.
And set about rebuilding.
And relearn joy.
As heroes toil.
And folk gather.
And layers wash.
And the roots of survivors grow strong
And deep.
And those who can't or can't imagine,
Move on.

And the earth assuredly ticks out time
While the shreds and shards of our sweet,
Wild mountain life are woven back together.
We're coming along. We've further to go.
Transformed. Transforming.
Like seed, shed in death but burrowed deep
And held close in upended river beds, we curl
Into our waiting and trust that creation's
Mandate is restoration.

Superheroes

Kara Dillow

Superheroes are ridiculous
And building unrealistic and impossible expectations of oneself
And creating a sense of reality and
thought patterns that will land most in
Therapy.
The rates of anxiety and depression are through the roof,
Due solely to delusions of grandeur.
Thanks Marvel.
Thanks Tic Tok.

We are humans,
And the concept of perfect is completely irrational.
Curse those who push it further,
Superhuman!

Fear not!
You are always somebody's idea
Of perfect.

Social Media and the internet
portray some of us as
Superheroes.
Do we want to see reality
Or just hope
For special powers
And do the really impossible?

We don't want to know that life is hard enough
Just as it is,
showing up every day,
jobs and paying bills,
Dragging a screaming child through the grocery store,
Returning to the same person every night,
Looking at the same you in the mirror everyday

With all the obvious imperfections,
Wrinkling and graying.
Bravery?
Strength?

Reality takes the most courage of all,
To walk out the door
With no delusions of grandeur,
As a humble human who simply believes that heroes don't have to be
Better than everyone.
They have to be just like everyone and still carry the groceries
And the sword.

Leap Of Faith

Susan Wiggin

I've heard it said that *"fear not"*
can be found 365 times in the Bible.
At least that's how I like to think of it:
spoken daily, by a Herald Angel,
and not as a suggestion.

"Be not afraid" is a miraculous message
delivered to ordinary humans:
To a virgin girl, when told she had been
chosen to carry God into the world;
To simple working folk, called to witness
that same newborn Messiah, and to
tell the world; And to all who
take that same leap past logic daily,
like me.

Ours is a brief and fearsome existence,
and we are walking bags of blood and
bone, so I find it reassuring that the
Author of it all wants us to know that
we don't need to fear. No. That we
are not to fear. Because He IS.
Emmanuel — God with us. God for us.
Such good news. Especially when
so much news is bad.

We have but to trust that. Trust Him.
Easier some days than others, if I'm
honest, and no doubt why there are
folks like me all over the world,
saying, "okay, so... how?"

Fear not. 365 days a year.

Kara Dillow has been writing since she was a teen: journaling, short stories, and poetry. She attended college in Boone, NC at Appalachian State University, where she began her Creative Writing path, and earned a BA in English with a minor in French. After college, Kara applied for several writing/editing jobs, but her choices in education led to her pivoting to the health and wellness industry. Kara received her Massage Therapy license in 2005 and completed her Classical Comprehensive Pilates training in 2010. She lives in Swannanoa, NC, where she and her husband are raising their two sons. Kara's husband works for a local solar company. Kara is the small business owner of a health and wellness company in East Asheville and spends her free time outside, playing with her family, traveling, reading, and sleeping.

Susan Wiggin — writer, designer, jazz singer, visual artist — curates, cultivates and reflects the permanent things of beauty and faith in her life and works. Relocating in 2020 from the Twin Cities of Minneapolis/St Paul to the Asheville area, Susan, a Boston native, graduated from the University of MA with a BA in Education/Human Services and from Hartford Seminary's Women's Leadership Institute. Following an early career in social work and then as creative director/designer/writer for her business communications firm, Susan now calls the Swannanoa River Valley home along with her husband, Doug, and Shiloh the Pretty Good Dane. Diverted by a pandemic, a move and a build, then surprised by a surprise hurricane which surprisingly required recalibration through poetry, Susan is now restored to work on her first novel, transformed by and more than ever grateful for God's illogical peace through every storm.

We would like to acknowledge our families for patiently waiting for us, and the locally owned and operated coffee shops between Asheville and Black Mountain, NC — especially *Filo Pastries* in East Asheville and *Peri Social House* in Black Mountain as well as *All Day Darling*, (the late, great) *Citizen Vinyl*, *Daymoon Coffeebar*, *Dripolator Coffee House*, *Dynamite Coffee*, *Flora Botanical Living*, *Recess Coffee + Baked Goods*, and *Sweeten Creek Coffee* — who provided for us safe space and good coffee throughout, even when water to make it was precious. And for Lauren Harr and Bobby Bradley — their wise, uplifting and professional guidance in launching this first publication of indie publisher *The Beacon Hill Project* — Susan is deeply grateful.

North Fork Reservoir

Bee Tree Reservoir

BLACK MOUNTAIN

SWANNANOA

Swannanoa River

EAST ASHEVILLE

To the French Broad River

www.ingramcontent.com/pod-product-compliance
Lightning Source LLC
Chambersburg PA
CBHW051635120626
46551CB00014B/2093